Sit & Solve
CROSS SUMS

MICHAEL RIOS

Sterling Publishing Co., Inc.
New York

Edited by Claire Bazinet

6 8 10 12 11 9 7 5

Published by Sterling Publishing Co., Inc.
387 Park Avenue South, New York, NY 10016
© 2003 by Michael Rios
Distributed in Canada by Sterling Publishing
% Canadian Manda Group, 165 Dufferin Street,
Toronto, Ontario, Canada M6K 3H6
Distributed in Great Britain by Chrysalis Books Group PLC,
The Chrysalis Building, Bramley Road, London W10 6SP, England
Distributed in Australia by Capricorn Link (Australia) Pty. Ltd.
P.O. Box 704, Windsor, NSW 2756, Australia

Sterling ISBN 0-8069-4413-7

For information about custom editions, special sales, premium and
corporate purchases, please contact Sterling Special Sales
Department at 800-805-5489 or specialsales@sterlingpub.com

CONTENTS

INTRODUCTION

The object of these puzzles is to fill in each of the blank squares with a digit from 1 to 9 so that no digit is repeated in a group of squares, and the sum of the digits in that group equals the clue number for that group. Let's solve an example to see how this is done:

Clues above the diagonal line are for groups of blank squares to the right; clues below the diagonal line are for groups of blank squares below. For example, the "7" at DF is the clue for the group made up of squares DG, DH, and DI.

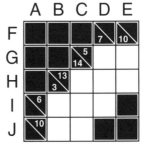

The "6" at AI can only be made with one set of numbers: 1, 2, and 3. (Experiment to verify that!) The "3" in that group can't be placed at BI; no number from 1 to 9 could be placed in BJ to make the clue "3" at BH true. The "3" can also not be placed at DI; do you see why? The "3," therefore, must be placed at CI.

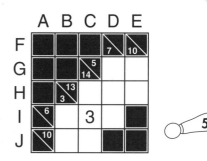

Now there are two possibilities for BI: "1" and "2." If BI = 1, then BJ = 2 (by the "3" clue at BH), CJ = 8 (by the "10" clue at AJ), and CH = 3 (by the "14" clue at CG). This puts two "3"s in the same group, which is not allowed....

So BI must be 2, BJ = 1, CJ = 9, and CH = 2. DI is forced to be 1. The clue at DF = 7; the only group that satifies that clue in three squares is 1, 2, and 4. Again, the 2 can't be at DH because no repeats are allowed.

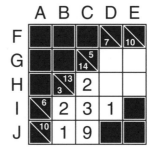

This means DG = 2, EG = 3, EH = 7, and DH = 4, which successfully completes this example puzzle.

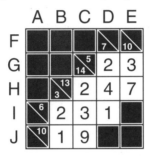

Keep working at these puzzles, and you will find many different tools to use to solve them successfully.

Good luck, and happy solving!

Mike Rios

About the Author

MIKE RIOS didn't invent the Cross Sums form but says "I've been doing these types of puzzles since I was a young lad in the mid 1970s."

Born and raised in Chicago, Michael Rios fell in love with math at St. Ignatius College Prep, and has been constructing puzzles in one way or another for the last 12 years or so. He works at the Chicago Board of Trade, and lives in Oswego, Illinois, with his wife, Theresa, and two children, Rebecca and Peter.

CROSS SUMS

PUZZLES

 9

Cross Sums #1

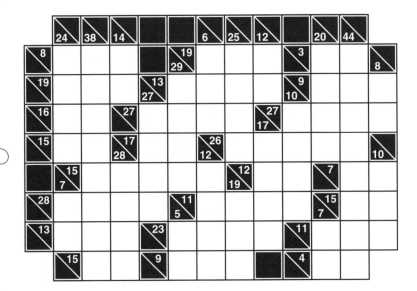

Answer on page 68.

Cross Sums #2

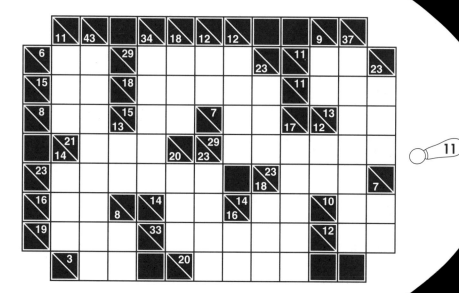

Answer on page 68.

Cross Sums #3

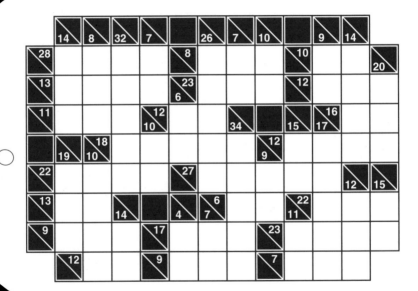

Answer on page 69.

Cross Sums #4

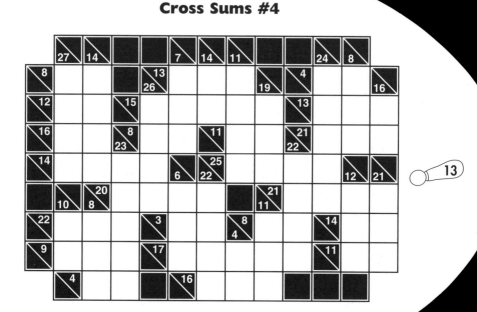

Answer on page 69.

13

Cross Sums #5

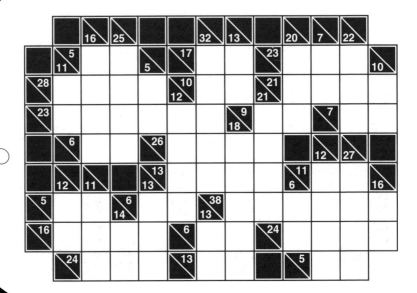

Answer on page 70.

Cross Sums #6

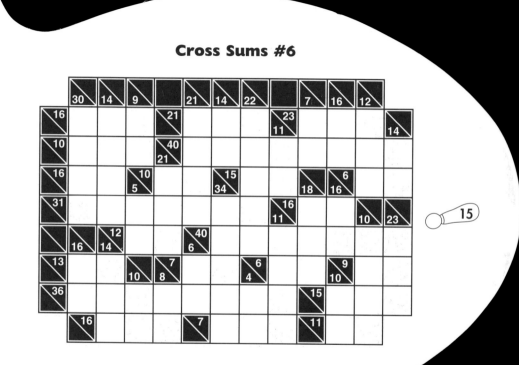

Answer on page 70.

Cross Sums #7

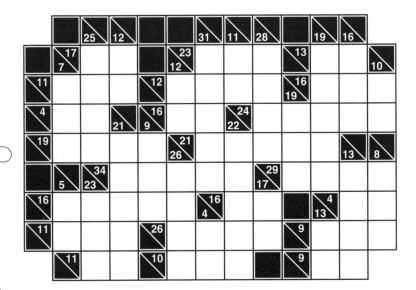

Answer on page 71.

Cross Sums #8

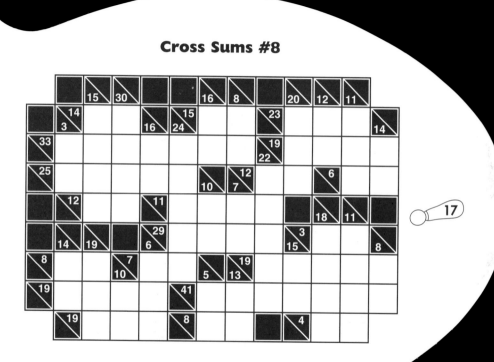

Answer on page 71.

Cross Sums #9

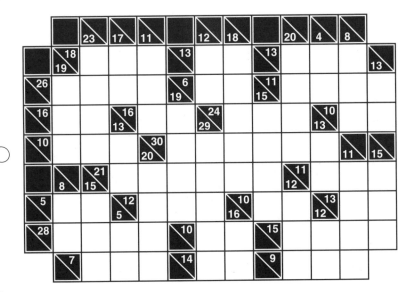

Answer on page 72.

Cross Sums #10

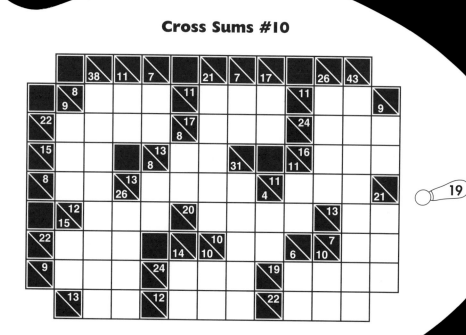

Answer on page 72.

19

Cross Sums #11

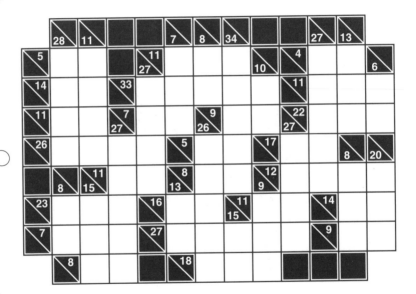

Answer on page 73.

20

Cross Sums #12

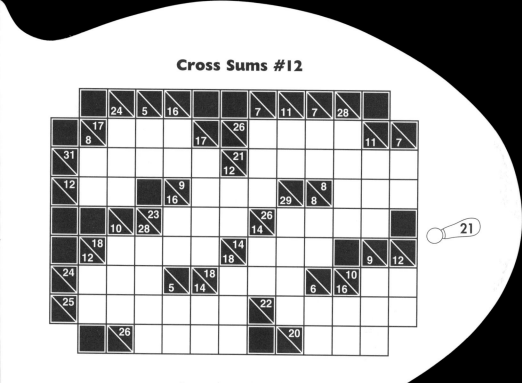

Answer on page 73.

21

Cross Sums #13

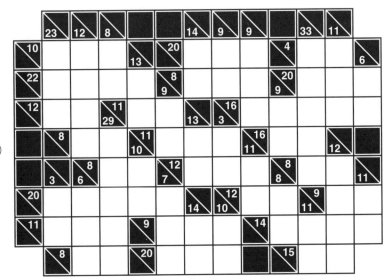

Answer on page 74.

Cross Sums #14

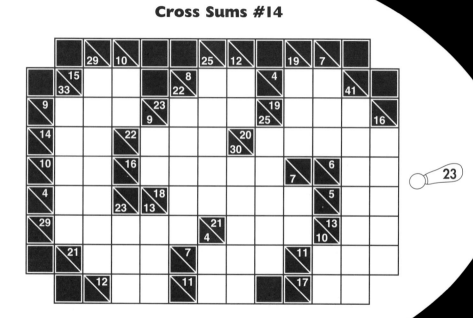

Answer on page 74.

Cross Sums #15

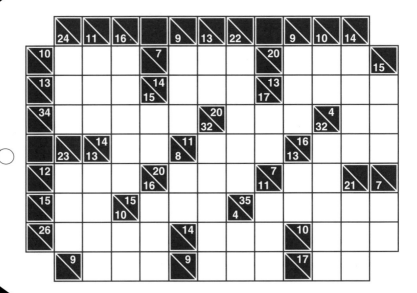

Answer on page 75.

Cross Sums #16

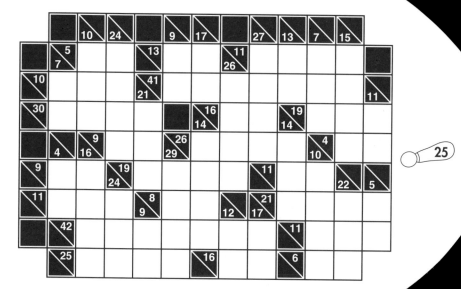

Answer on page 75.

Cross Sums #17

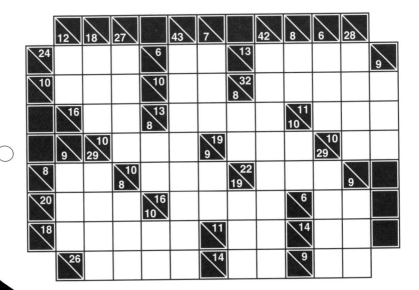

Answer on page 76.

Cross Sums #18

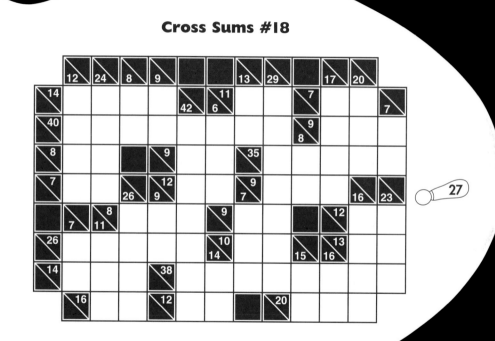

27

Answer on page 76.

Cross Sums #19

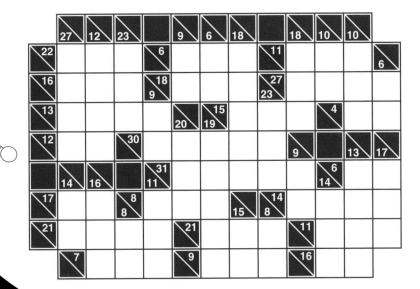

Answer on page 77.

Cross Sums #20

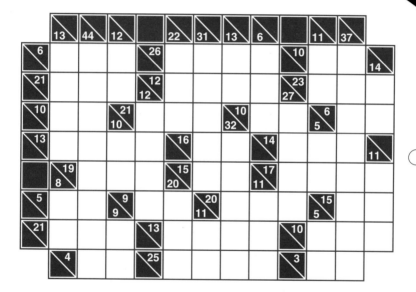

29

Answer on page 77.

Cross Sums #21

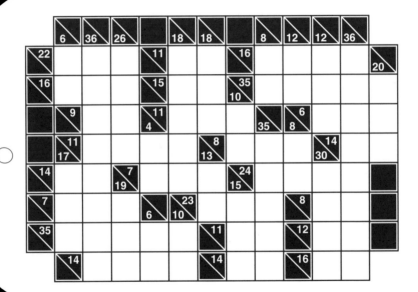

Answer on page 78.

Cross Sums #22

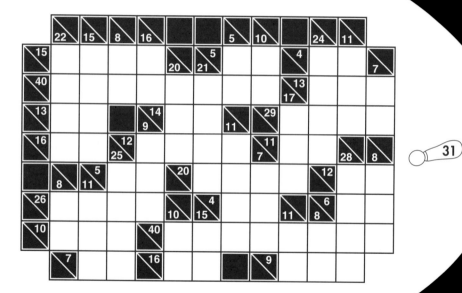

Answer on page 78.

Cross Sums #23

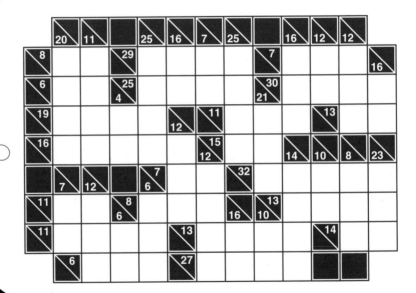

Answer on page 79.

Cross Sums #24

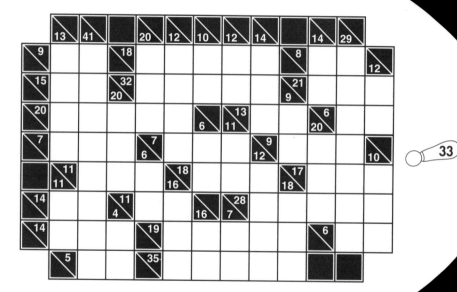

Answer on page 79.

Cross Sums #25

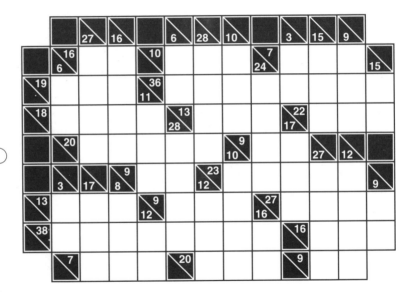

Answer on page 80.

Cross Sums #26

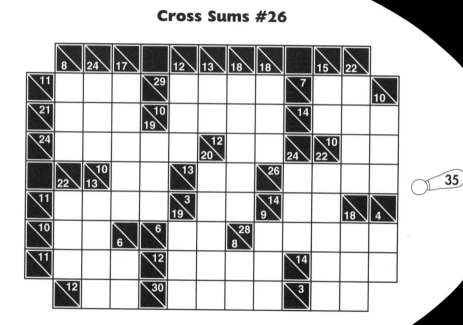

Answer on page 80.

35

Cross Sums #27

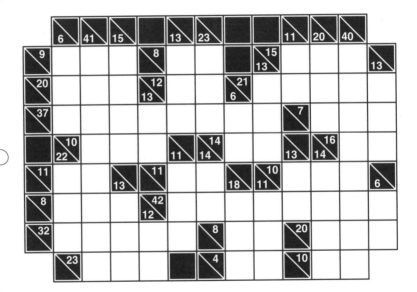

Answer on page 81.

36

Cross Sums #28

Answer on page 81.

Cross Sums #29

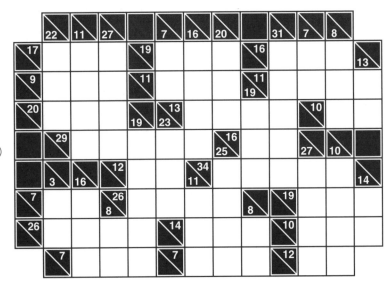

Answer on page 82.

Cross Sums #30

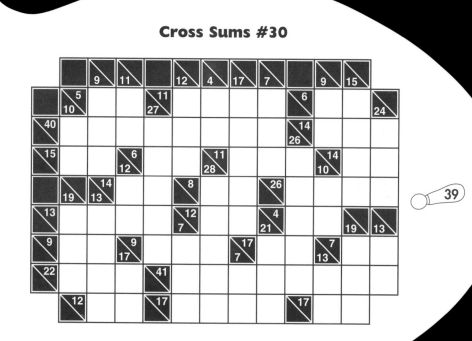

Answer on page 82.

Cross Sums #31

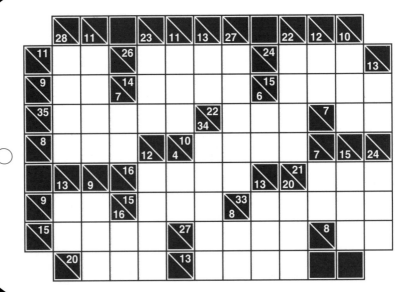

Answer on page 83.

Cross Sums #32

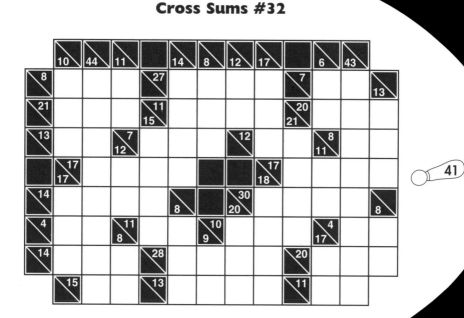

Answer on page 83.

Cross Sums #33

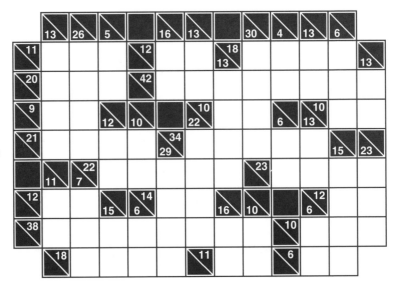

Answer on page 84.

Cross Sums #34

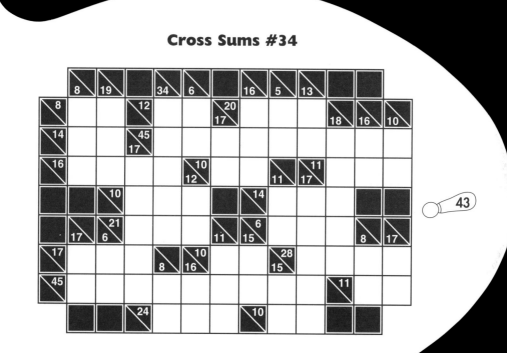

Answer on page 84.

Cross Sums #35

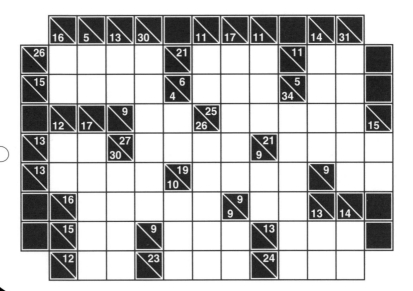

Answer on page 85.

Cross Sums #36

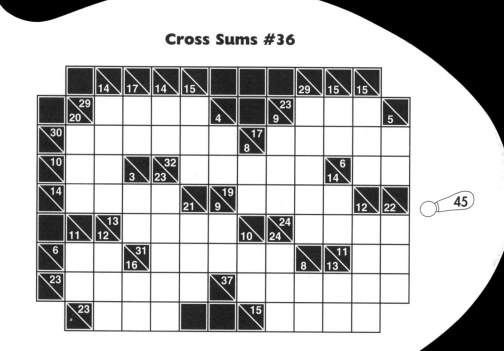

Answer on page 85.

Cross Sums #37

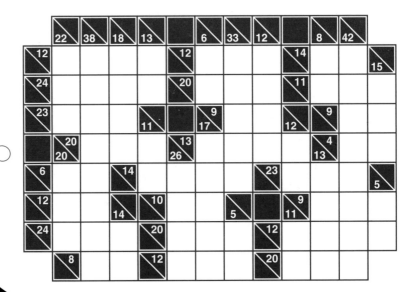

46

Answer on page 86.

Cross Sums #38

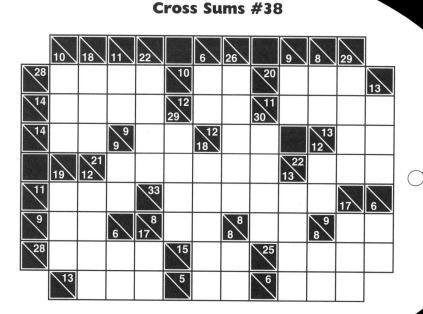

Answer on page 86.

Cross Sums #39

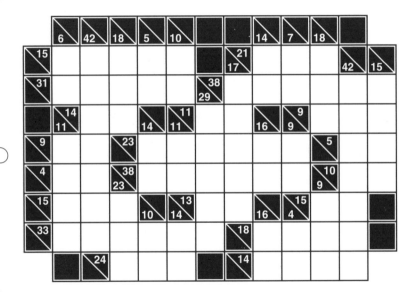

Answer on page 87.

48

Cross Sums #40

49

Answer on page 87.

Cross Sums #41

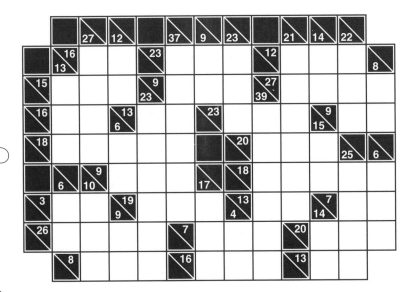

Answer on page 88.

Cross Sums #42

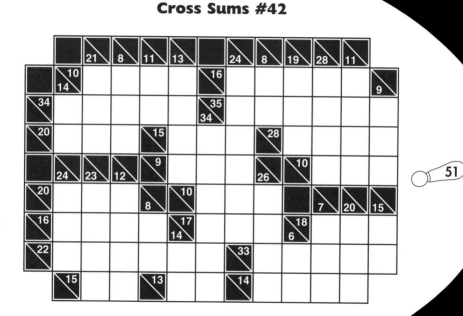

Answer on page 88.

Cross Sums #43

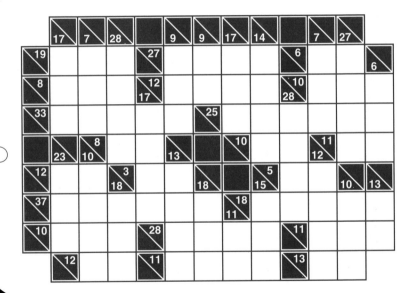

Answer on page 89.

Cross Sums #44

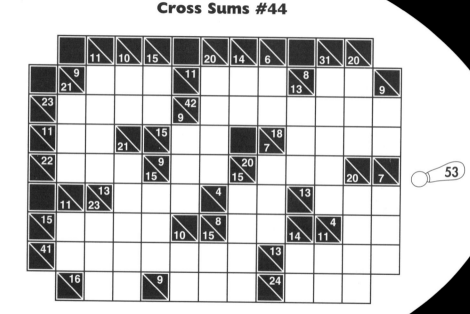

Answer on page 89.

Cross Sums #45

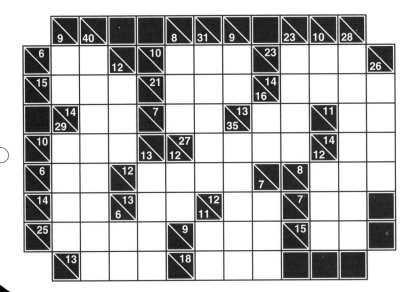

54

Answer on page 90.

Cross Sums #46

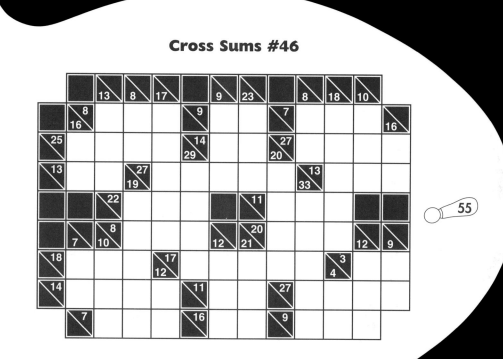

55

Answer on page 90.

Cross Sums #47

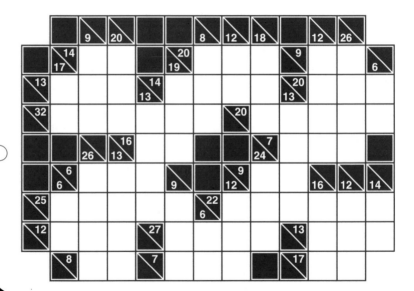

56

Answer on page 91.

Cross Sums #48

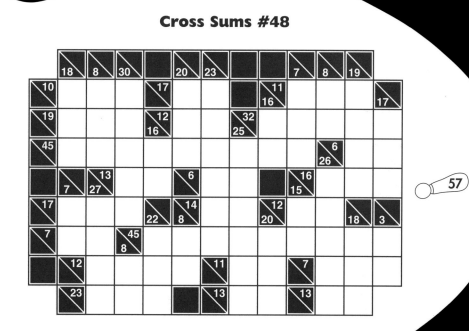

57

Answer on page 91.

Cross Sums #49

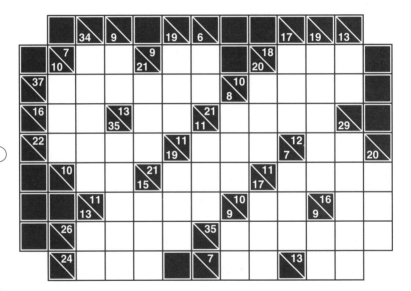

Answer on page 92.

Cross Sums #50

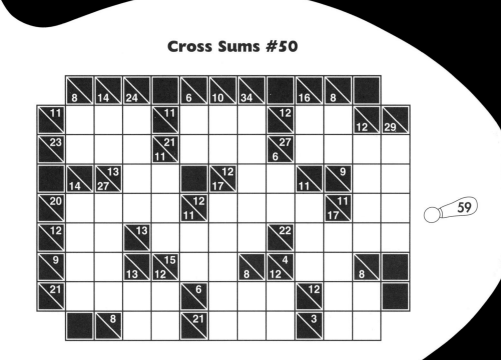

59

Answer on page 92.

Cross Sums #51

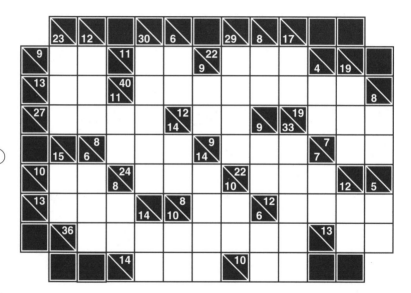

60

Answer on page 93.

Cross Sums #52

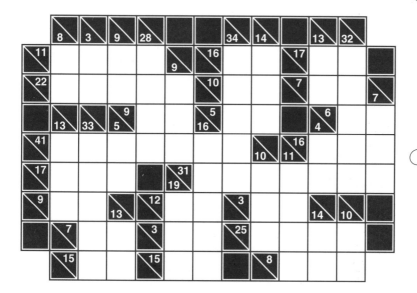

Answer on page 93.

Cross Sums #53

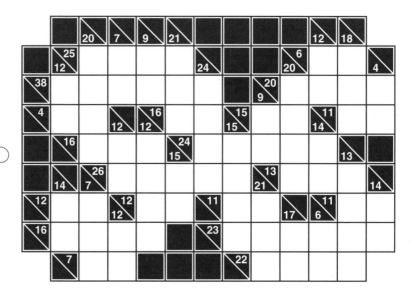

Answer on page 94.

Cross Sums #54

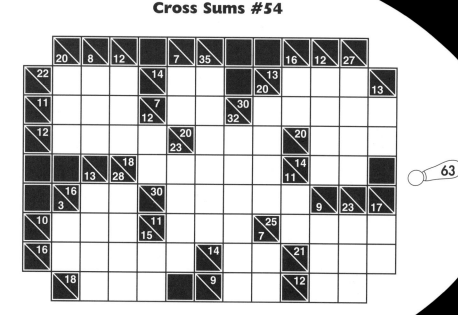

63

Answer on page 94.

Cross Sums #55

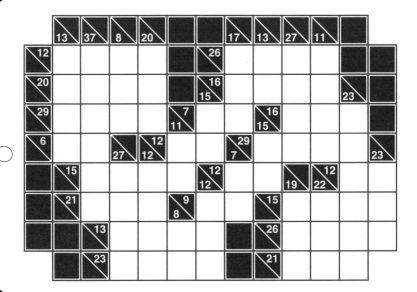

Answer on page 95.

Cross Sums #56

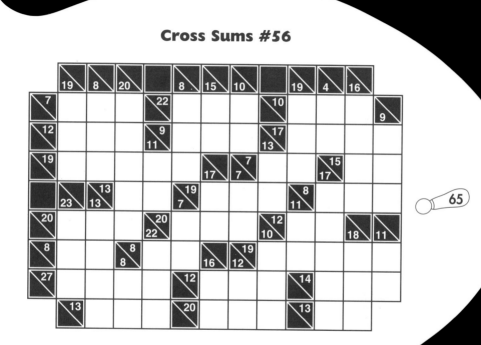

Answer on page 95.

Cross Sums #57

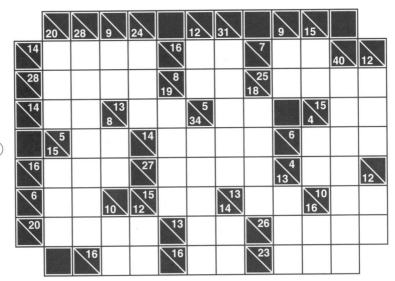

Answer on page 96.

Cross Sums #58

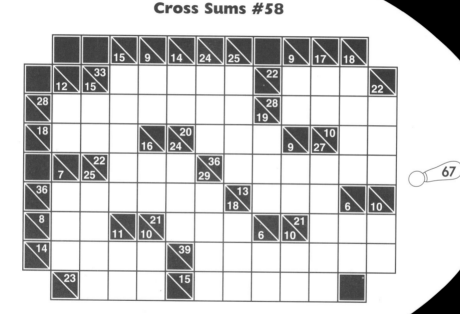

67

Answer on page 96.

A N S W E R S

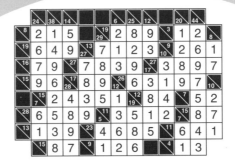

#1

#2

#3

#4

69

#5

#6

70

#7

	25	12			31	11	28		19	16	
17\7	9	8		23\12	6	9	8	13\	5	8	\10
11\	2	5	4	12\	5	1	2	4	16\19	3	7	6
4\	1	3	21\	16\9	7	9	24\22	9	8	2	1	4
19\	4	8	5	2	21\26	8	3	7	2	1	13\ 8\
5\ 34\23	9	6	8	7	4	29\17	9	8	7	5
16\	3	6	4	1	2	16\4	7	9		4\13	3	1
11\	2	8	1	26\	9	3	6	8	9\	6	1	2
11\	9	2	10\	7	1	2		9\	7	2

#8

	15	30			16	8		20	12	11	
14\3	6	8	16\	15\24	9	6	23\	6	9	8	14\
33\	1	3	6	9	5	7	2	19\22	5	3	2	9
25\	2	1	9	7	6	10\ 12\7	3	9	6\	1	5
12\	5	7	11\	1	3	2	5		18\ 11\
14\ 19\			29\6	8	7	5	9	15\3	1	2	8\
8\	5	3	7\10	3	4	5\ 19\13	1	8	5	3	2
19\	9	7	2	1	41\	2	8	4	7	9	5	6
19\	9	8	2		3	5		4\	3	1

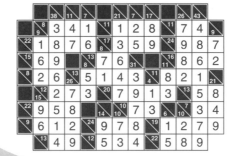

#9

#10

72

#11

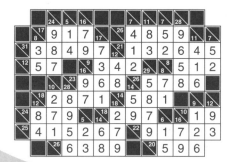

#12

#13

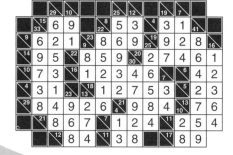

#14

#15

	24\	11\	16\		9\	13\	22\		9\	10\	14\	
\10	7	1	2	\7	1	4	2	\20	3	9	8	\15
\13	8	2	3	\14\15	2	9	3	\13\17	2	1	3	7
\34	9	8	4	7	6	\20\32	7	9	4	\4\32	1	3
	\23\14\13	6	8	\11\8	2	1	8	\16\13	9	2	5
\12	9	2	1	\20\16	3	8	9	\7\11	4	3	\21	
\15	8	7	\15\10	1	5	9	\35\4	5	9	7	8	6
\26	6	3	8	\14	7	3	4	\10	5	4	1	
	\9	1	2	6	\9	6	1	2	\17	8	9	

#16

		10\	24\		9\	17\		27\	13\	7\	15\	
	\5\7	1	4	\13	5	8	\11\26	3	5	1	2	
\10	1	2	7	\41\21	4	9	6	7	8	2	5	\11
\30	6	7	8	9		\16\14	7	9	\19\14	4	7	8
\4	\9\16	5	4	\26\29	7	9	8	2	\4\10	1	3	
\9	3	6	\19\24	8	5	2	4	\11	7	4	\22	\5
\11	1	2	8	\8\9	7	1	\21\17	5	3	9	4	
	\42	3	7	6	9	4	5	8	\11	2	8	1
	\25	5	9	3	8	\16	7	9	\6	1	5	

#17

#18

76

#19

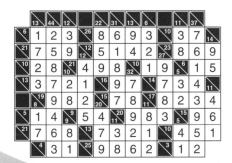

#20

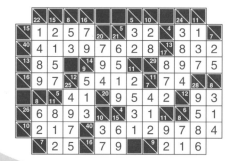

#21

#22

78

#23

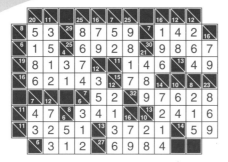

#24

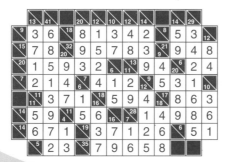

#25

	27\	16\			6\	28\	10\		3\	15\	9\
\16 6\	9	7	\10	1	6	3	7\24	2	4	1	\15
19\	5	8	6	36\11	5	8	6	4	1	2	3	7
18\	1	7	2	8	13\28	9	1	3	22\17	9	5	8
\20	3	1	2	9	5	9\10	8	1	27\	12\	
3\ 17\	9\8	1	8	23\12	2	9	7	4	1	\9	
13\	1	9	3	9\12	6	2	1	27\16	9	8	6	4
38\	2	6	4	8	5	1	3	9	16\	9	2	5
\7	2	1	4	\20	9	4	7	\9	6	3	

#26

	8\	24\	17\		12\	13\	18\	18\		15\	22\
11\	1	7	3	29\	8	9	5	7	7\	6	1	10\
21\	5	9	7	10\19	3	4	1	2	14\	9	4	1
24\	2	8	4	9	1	12\20	3	9	24\	10\22	8	2
22\	13\	2	8	13\	6	7	26\	8	2	9	7
11\	5	3	1	2	19\	1	2	14\	9	5	18\	4\
10\	9	1	6\	6\	4	2	28\8	1	7	8	9	3
11\	8	2	1	12\	6	3	1	2	14\	6	7	1
\12	7	5	30\	9	8	7	6	\3	1	2	

80

#27

	6\	41\	15\		13\	23\		11\	20\	40\	
9\	1	6	2	8\	2	6	15\13	5	9	1	13\
20\	3	9	8	12\13	4	8	21\6	1	6	7	4	3
37\	2	5	4	6	7	9	1	3	7\	4	2	1
22\10	2	1	7	11\	14\	5	9	13\	16\14	7	9
11\	8	3	13\	11\	2	9	18\	10\11	6	1	3	6\
8\	5	1	2	42\12	1	5	9	8	7	4	6	2
32\	9	7	5	3	8	8\	6	2	20\	7	9	4
23\	8	6	9		4\	3	1	10\	2	8

#28

	12\	15\		28\	23\	9\	8\		28\	19\	
7\	1	6	26\	8	9	7	2	5\	1	4	14\
16\	4	3	9	11\	5	3	2	1	16\11	3	8	5
8\	2	6	20\	16\23	9	7	35\	5	6	8	7	9
26\	1	2	5	8	6	4	26\	8\13	1	7	25\	6\
4\	14\15	8	6	12\	27\	3	1	4	9	8	2
29\	3	5	4	9	8	13\16	9	4	7\14	6	1
6\	1	3	2	16\	1	7	6	2	19\	9	7	3
8\	7	1	26\	3	9	8	6	9\	5	4

#28

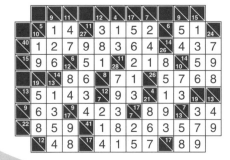

#29

#30

82

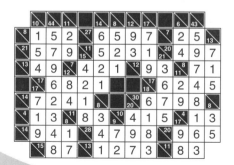

#31

#32

#33

#34

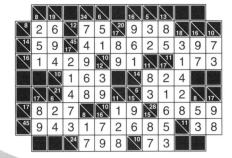

#35

16	5	13	30		11	17	11		14	31
9	3	8	6	9	4	8		3	8	
7	2	5	1	2	3	1		1	4	
		8	1	1	2	5	8	9		
9	4	9	3	8	7		3	2	7	9
3	1	7	2	1	2	7	9		3	6
2	6	4	1	3		2	7			
7	8		3	5	1		2	6	5	
3	9	6	9	8		8	7	9		

#36

	14	17	14	15				29	15	15
7	9	8	5			8	9	6		
9	4	8	6	2	1	1	2	6	5	
8	2		8	3	7	5	9		4	2
3	1	2	8		1	3	6	9		
	1	3	7	2		4	5	6	9	
5	1	4	9	7	3	8		3	8	
6	3	7	2	5	7	9	6	8	2	5
8	9	6			7	2	5	1		

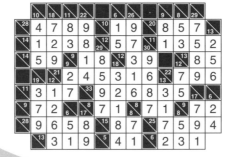

#37

#38

86

#39

#40

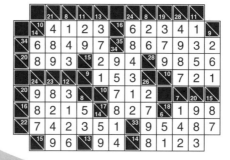

#41

#42

88

#43

#44

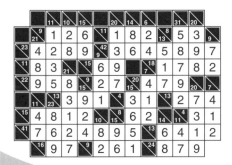

#45

Clues (top): 9\40 · 8\31\9 · 23\10\28

Row 1: 6\ 2 4 | 12\10\ 1 7 2 | 23\ 9 8 6 | 26\
Row 2: 15\ 7 3 5 | 21\ 5 9 7 | 14\16 7 2 1 4
Row 3: 14\29 8 6 | 7\ 2 5 | 35\13 9 4 | 11\ 3 8
Row 4: 10\ 7 2 1 | 13\27\12 8 9 7 3 | 14\12 5 9
Row 5: 6\ 5 1 | 12\ 1 4 2 5 | 7\ 8\ 1 2 5
Row 6: 14\ 8 6 | 13\6 5 8 | 12\11 8 4 | 7\ 3 4
Row 7: 25\ 9 7 5 4 | 9\ 2 6 1 | 15\ 8 7
Row 8: 13\ 9 1 3 | 18\ 9 7 2

#46

Clues (top): 13\8\17 · 9\23 · 8\18\10

Row 1: 8\16 4 1 3 | 9\ 1 8 | 7\ 1 2 4 | 16\
Row 2: 25\ 9 3 7 6 | 14\29 5 9 | 27\20 7 6 5 9
Row 3: 13\ 7 6 | 27\19 1 8 3 6 9 | 13\33 5 1 7
Row 4: 22\ 8 5 9 | 11\ 3 7 1 |
Row 5: 7\10\8 1 2 5 | 12\20\21 7 9 4 | 12\9\
Row 6: 18\ 6 7 5 | 17\12 7 2 4 1 3 | 3\4 1 2
Row 7: 14\ 1 2 3 8 | 11\ 3 8 | 27\ 8 3 9 7
Row 8: 7\ 1 2 4 | 16\ 7 9 | 6 1 2

90

#47

	9	20			8	12	18		12	26	
14\17	5	9		20\	3	8	9	9\	2	7	6\
\13	8	1	4	14\13	2	1	4	7	6	9	5
\32	9	3	7	1	8	4	\20	2	6	3	1
	26\	13\	7	9			\7\24	4	1	2	
\6\6	3	1	2		9\	9\12	8	1	16\	12\	14\
\25	5	9	7	3	1	22\6	1	7	2	4	3
\12	1	8	3	27\	6	5	7	9	13\	3	1
\8	6	2		\7	2	1	4		17\	9	8

#48

	18	8	30		20	23		7	8	19	
10\	4	1	5	17\	9	8	\11\16	1	2	8	17\
19\	8	2	9	12\16	8	4	\32\25	9	2	6	7
45\	6	5	8	9	3	1	2	7	4	\6\26	1	5
\7\27	13\	6	7	\6	2	4		16\15	9	3	4
17\	6	9	2	14\22	5	9	12\20	9	3	18\	3\
\7	1	6	\45\8	8	7	3	1	5	6	4	9	2
\12	4	2	5	1	11\	3	8	\7	2	4	1
\23	8	6	9		13\	6	7	13\	8	5	

91

#49

#50

#51

#52

#53

#54

#55

#56

#57

#58

96